LEARNING
HAPPENS
THROUGH
CONVERSATIONS

5 LEADERSHIP LESSONS FOR MASTERFUL LIVING

L. KOBIE DA WIZ

For bulk orders, speaking engagements, or leadership coaching,
contact us at info@lkobiedawiz.com.

ISBN: 978-1-947490-10-9

Cover design: De'Aris Ferguson
Book design: Aaron J. Ratzlaff

Please visit us at the official website
www.lkobiedawiz.com

To Carolyn,

I hope this moves you 3 shifts you in a way you were never expecting. Thank you for being who you are!

L. Kobe DaWiz

2/2021

DEDICATION

This book is dedicated to the people who have something inside of them, and they don't really know how to get it out. My hope is this book forces you to have conversations with yourself and others that open up perspectives, ideas, and possibilities you never thought possible to make that thing inside you manifest. My sincere prayer is this becomes a tool to help you create the interactions needed to unleash all that's inside of you. This book is dedicated to you!

CONTENTS

ACKNOWLEDGEMENTS

I want to thank Tee and April for 25 years of friendship. I appreciate the last 6-7 years of working together as a team. Thanks for being champions for EVERY project I embark on, and doing your best to keep me on track and focused (It's a real job). I appreciate the encouragement and the criticism. I know both of you come from an honest and genuine space of working to pull the best out of me.

I want to sincerely thank my friend and fraternity brother Craig King who sacrificed his time and energy to make sure I stayed true to what was coming through me, and gave me amazing feedback EVERY step of the way. This project was made better because of your meaningful cooperation and your willingness to give freely of yourself. I'm beyond grateful. Friendship is Essential to the Soul.

I want to thank my small circle of friends who I called to tell them I had to write a book in seven days, and they gave me nothing but encouragement and confidence. You know who you are.
(A.B., L.W., and C.J.)

Lastly, I want to thank my wife Ashlye for your loving support and willingness to take on the girls and keep them engaged, and distracted over these 7 days from playing with Daddy. I'm thankful for your love. I want to thank Alana(6) and Ariah(3) for doing your best to give me the room to complete this heavy assignment in what was a very busy week.

INTRODUCTION

LIFE ITSELF IS A DIFFICULT JOURNEY! There are many ways one can choose to live and none of them are necessarily the "right way" or the "wrong way." But, what you MUST do is figure out YOUR way(s) to live your life. I am starting to write this book as I lay in my bed Saturday August 22nd, 2020, exactly 89 (or 90 depending on how you count) days until my 44th birthday on November 19th. The significance of that, I don't quite know yet, but the Universe/Spirit/God/Allah/Jesus, or however and whoever you recognize as being, ALL in ALL, let me know there is importance in it, and I clearly heard that I am to be done with this book by next Friday August 28th. So, I was given 7 days to write this book (something I've never done before). Now I know that 7 is the number of completion, which is why I'm guessing I have only been given 7 days. I don't know why I am hearing so clearly. But, I am thankful and grateful that I have been selected to bring you all whatever is about to come through me. My prayer and hope is it blesses you and gives you something that will aid you in living your life more powerfully. The power and the tools you need to live your life as you desire resides in and around you. I just opened my Facebook and I'm being spoken to again …

(Morning Message on 8/22/18)

You take the test till you pass! The reason the same things are showing up in your life is because you haven't passed the test! Life is designed to create a better you. If you're not getting better, then you don't get to move on to the next thing. There is NO social promotion! So, you don't get to move on just because you've gotten older. You don't do the work required then you don't get to pass! Take a moment and see what keeps showing up that's keeping you from living your best life and alter your behavior and actions. Learn your lessons so you can get promoted! Self-reflection is part of the lesson! DO what you know so you can grow!

#italktomyself #grownpeoplestuff #morningmotivation #lkobiedawiz #leadfromwithin #kobiespeaks #learnyourlessons #lkobiedawizcoaching #powerliving #wizism

So, this is for sure a test and I'm definitely going to pass. I'm excited about what this is going to pull out of me, and I know one of the lessons is recognizing what's in you isn't just for you, but for others too.

8/28/20- Introduction Addition.

I finished this book in the seven-day time frame. I was instructed I could not add anymore to the body of the book. I could only add to the introduction, and the "Day 8 Notes" you'll find at the end of the book. As you read this book, I believe you will find it helpful to stop at the end of each chapter and pull out your lessons learned and your takeaways. I know it may seem a bit much, but I promise as you read the next chapter it will be helpful for you to refer back to. As you end the book, you will find yourself with helpful lessons and takeaways. Secondly, I want you to think about what you can apply to your life. This is an easy read, but reading it definitely is going to unlock something in you. I know because as I went back and read, the shift in me was meaningful. You received this book exactly as it came through me. There was very little editing done on purpose to maintain the voices of both characters. If you find a few errors that I missed, charge it to me seeking to keep the integrity of the message as I received it. When you get ready to read this book, it will probably serve you to be in a quiet place and have a notepad ready to receive what is going to be spoken to you. I KNOW it's going to happen because there is an energy tied to this book that HAS to come through! And, as you read the conversations that are taking place, there is a conversation that is going to begin on the inside of you, and you need to be ready to listen and respond. I can say that with confidence because after being the vessel for this book I know I DID NOT WRITE this book. It was my

3

experiences, and I was the one to put pen to paper. But, I was merely a vessel used to deliver the message. This book is for some really special people and if you are reading it count yourself to be one of them. This was a message that HAD to get out, and I was only the messenger. Be blessed, be ready, and most importantly be open to receive what is for YOU.

WIZISM

"You take the test till you pass! The reason the same things are showing up in your life is because you haven't passed the test!"

WIZISM

"You HAVE to make your
main competition yourself!"

CHAPTER 1

Stay in *Your* Lane and Run *Your* Race!

HAVE YOU EVER BEEN IN WHAT YOU THOUGHT was a perfect situation on your journey of success only to find out that it really wasn't that perfect at all? In 2004 I moved to Atlanta, Georgia to make a fresh start. Prior to moving to Atlanta, I was successfully teaching in Topeka, Kansas. I was selected to be one of two interns among a cohort of nine who completed a district leadership-training program and was awarded an assistant principal position. I was excited and humbled, to say the least. I worked extremely hard over those 20 weeks to make sure I was going to get one of those two positions. I sat with the associate superintendent who told me I finished at the top and would have my choice of the two assistant principal positions. She stated she saw a great deal of promise in me and guaranteed me I would be given my own school after one year and would probably be the youngest principal the district had ever had. I was flattered and ecstatic! I had to put those feelings on pause because I knew I had to bring up some concerns and issues I noticed and felt needed to be addressed while going through the internship. I pulled out my notebook and went down my list. She listened attentively. She nodded her head as I spoke and when I finished, she commenced to say, "Thanks for sharing that with me. Now, in which of the two schools would you like to begin your administrative career?" I paused. I thought about it for a moment and then I said, "I think I'm going to resign." She said, "What?!" Loudly in my head, I said, "What the heck did I just say?" I took a breath and paused again. I then said it a bit more emphatically, "Yeah, I think I'm going to resign." She looked as if I somewhat offended her. "Is it money? We can possibly come up a little more if that's the issue." I looked her in her eyes and said, "No ma'am, it's not that at all. I just think the path that I'm traveling on is now causing for a drastic change of course." She looked at me puzzled, and in a noticeably confused tone said, "Really?! What are you going to do?" I continued my staring into her eyes and sat up as straight as I could and with as much confidence as I could pull from within me and said, "I'm going to move to Atlanta and start my own consulting company." She leaned forward intrigued, "Wow! How are you going to do that?" I sat back confidently and said, "I don't have a clue, but I am definitely going to figure it out." She leaned back too and said, "There is no doubt in my mind, Mr. Wilkerson, that you will. Well, if you ever decide to come back here just know there is always a place in USD 501 for you." I stood up, shook her hand, and reached down and grabbed my briefcase and planner. I left her office feeling super strong and extremely terrified all at the same time. Self-doubt IMMEDIATELY started whispering in my ear after walking out the door, "Have you lost your mind? What are you doing? Are you sure that was a smart thing to do?" So, I opened my mouth spoke back to it and said, "I trust me, and I am capable and able to create and cultivate the future I want. I believe in me and my skills and abilities!" You know all those questions that start flooding your mind like a river overflowing its banks: What are you going to do for work? How are you going to make money? What do you know about consulting? What are you going to offer? And many, many more questions to aid in building uncertainty and fear kept coming. I just kept saying aloud to myself "I believe in me and my skills and abilities!" You have to be very careful what you allow to take root in your mind because you'll make thoughtful calculated decisions and then talk yourself right out of the same decisions YOU just made, which you know are in your best interest. You don't always get to choose the thoughts that come into your mind, but you do get to choose what stays. You'll be quick and decisive and then you'll waver and recoil because you're scared and feel like you don't have all the answers. It's at THAT moment you MUST recognize your faith is being tested, and you MUST pass the test! Your poised intentional position is to stand strong, and exercise an unwavering faith in yourself and in whatever you're believing in or going after. Not having all the answers and not clearly seeing the end of a thing is par for the course when stepping out into the unknown. A faith that can be seen and touched really isn't faith at all; and a faith that hasn't been tested is a faith that can't be trusted! Trust in you, and what comes through you, so your faith can be a faith that you can trust! It's not UNTIL you step out into your Red Sea that it will become dry land.

Once in Atlanta, I began to recognize the people and the energy of this place was a lot different than any other place I'd lived before. There was a productiveness and a determination that was infectious and inspiring. It made me think OutKast and the ATLiens may have been more than just an album title. I mean literally the first 4-6 weeks I was there it was like everyone lived there but nobody was from there. And everyone I met had at least 2-3 things they did. And if you did not have multiple ways of earning income, you were looked at a little strange. I didn't have a job and was figuring out my way. So, I would be out in the middle of the day meeting and networking with people. The conversation would go something like, "Hey how are you doing and what do you do?" and I say feeling proud of myself, "I just moved here and I'm working on starting up my own educational consulting company." "Aw man that's fire, I wish you the best with that. So, what else you do?" I'm like, bruh, didn't you just hear me say I'm trying to start a whole company over here? And I'd say, "That's all I'm doing right now. I'm putting all my focus and energy in that." "Oh ok, but you might want to think about getting some other hustles. Somebody 'gon' make this money it might as well be you." Then they'd let me know how many hustles they had. They weren't bragging or boasting, just sharing their life with me. It was these many encounters that let me know that I needed to diversify my skillset and hone my talents, so I had more than one tool in my tool belt to work with.

While in Atlanta I had A LOT of hustles and learned so many ways to make money. I had some jobs I thought I would never have. I was a fleet supervisor for a guy who had a mobile fleet service and a detail company. I changed oil, installed brakes, put decals on trucks, and managed employees and contracts. I learned from him the importance of maintaining relationships and not having to be the smartest person in the room. He was from California and his wife was a surgeon and she made over 400K a year, so he really didn't have to work. But, he liked the hustle and bustle of business and understood how to talk to people, and enjoyed the game, and the chase of making money. Watching and listening to him, I learned to negotiate, and learned strategies and systems to disarm hostile people and help them to relax and let down their barriers. While he was amazing with talking to clients he was just as drastically non-amazing when it came to managing and talking to his employees. He had a temper that was unbelievable! How can you be so skilled at talking to one group of people and yet so unskilled at talking to another group? Leading people simply was not his thing, and even though he wasn't the perfect boss, I saw what I could learn from working with him. I eventually had to release myself from that assignment, but I left with a lot of tangible lessons and felt like I added to him, and his company as well. I also sold ADT security systems door to door in new housing developments. This definitely helped me cultivate some real tough skin, as well as taught me how to connect to strangers and not look or feel like a creep who was casing their house to rob them. I was part of consumer study groups that would have you try on different protective equipment or taste new products, and so on. Those experiences would pay like $100 to as high as $350 for 3-4 hours of your time. I was constantly made aware of the variety of traditional and non-traditional ways of earning income. It was these experiences that further solidified my belief that my skills and abilities would provide for me. What I needed was a picture of a process to show me how to maximize what I already had.

I sat down and had a conversation with an orthopedic surgeon that shifted my whole way of thinking. It really let me know there are levels to this life thing, and you have to be aware of the perspectives of different people. It's the same game, but the level at which people engage and participate are not the same. So, I became part of a mastermind group that met at 6am twice a month for one hour and included every level of people you can imagine. There were people like me who were just starting out, people who were making 100K a year, 400K a year, 1Million, 3-4Million, and upwards of 10Million. It was a blessing to be a part of that group because it showed me more than anything these successful people weren't any different than me. EXCEPT they thought differently and their level of risk vs. reward was greater than mine.

I sat down and wanted to discuss my goals with someone who I considered successful and was earning A LOT more than me. My hope was to gain an alternative life perspective, and some advice that would propel me to the next level in my thinking and living. You never know what or how certain experiences or conversations will move you or propel you forward. So, I sat down with him, and thanked him for his time and told him I just wanted to have a casual but intentional conversation, and any advice he could give me would be welcomed. I told him my story, and how I arrived at this present moment in my life and monetarily where I was trying to go. He listened to me and then he looked at me and paused. He sat back and folded his arms, and then he sat up, leaned forward, and pointed at me and said, "You know what? I don't know if you recognize it or not, but you're focused on competing against others and trying to better them, or outperform them. And while some people find success there, I don't believe that perspective or path to be the most beneficial motivator or sustainer of long-term success. You HAVE to make your main competition yourself; and here's why. Let's say you're trying to be the number 1 salesman or the top person in any field. You'll naturally look at the current person in the spot you're going after and consider them to be your competition. You may study what they are doing and model their work ethic and do your best to figure out how you can get where they are. And you should! But you shouldn't. You have to realize your path and the way you may go about doing the same thing they are doing possibly, and most likely is going to be different. AND most importantly, when you get to the number 1 spot and surpass them, who then will be your competition? That's why you always have to try to beat yourself! That way you're guaranteed to always win. Now let me be clear when I say there's definitely habits, behaviors, and character traits that are consistent with successful people across the board. Those things are no secret. Tenacity, perseverance, discipline, hard work, consistency, follow-through, open-mindedness, being teachable, focus, vision, and I can go on. But, I'm not telling you anything that you don't already know. What you and a lot of other people don't REALLY know is your secret sauce and magical ingredient in putting together your potion of success is YOU, and your strong belief in your skills and abilities." I'm thinking, hey I know that! That is exactly what I told myself when doubt tried to enter my mind when I walked away from the position in Kansas, but I didn't say it out loud. I just continued listening. He leaned forward as he kept talking. "Now, I know you're probably thinking to yourself: I know that! And you're thinking I definitely believe in myself." At this point in the conversation, I'm like whoa, this dude is good; did he hear me think that? Then he paused and looked intently at me and put his hands together in a praying posture. Then collapsed his bottom three fingers on each other and his index fingers and thumbs formed the shape of a gun pointed at the ceiling. He moved his hands toward his face where his chin landed on his thumbs, and tapped his nose twice with his two index fingers and then he pointed at me and said, "But do you really?!" I didn't know if it was a rhetorical question or if he was really waiting for me to answer, and I didn't want to stop his flow, so I just looked back at him and nodded slowly. He then said, "I mean your belief in you has to be unshakeable to the point where it may almost be perceived as arrogance. I mean so strong that doubt and thoughts of doubt don't even enter your mind. Many people look at surgeons and think we're arrogant, or buttholes, or arrogant buttholes and we're not. Well most of us aren't anyway." He chuckled. "It's simply a confidence we MUST possess because we literally have people's lives in our hands when we operate on them, and there is NO ROOM for doubt when we have tools in our hands where one wrong move can end life. We have to know the move we're making is the right one and no one can tell us any different because we have researched, studied, prepared, learned and we trust ourselves. We know what we know and have confidence in our abilities more than anyone or anything else. So much so the only thing we see is the achieving of whatever we're going after or the accomplishment of what we're doing. That's the level of belief I'm talking about! That's how you have to live your life." I looked at him nodding and said, "So, losing or failing is not an option?" He sat up quickly and pounded his fist on the desk and slightly raised his voice, "No! It's so much more than that! It's deeper than a quickly spoken cliché! It's you're so focused you literally NEVER give a thought to the outcome being anything other than what you anticipated and prepared for. To say losing or failing is not an option means that the thought of losing or failing at some point had to come across your mind. I'm talking about a level of thinking and living that has been created and cultivated in you where the idea of losing or failing or what you're after not working does not even have space to live inside of your mind for even a millisecond. A level of commitment so strong you literally persuade the universe to bend towards your will. So narrow is your focus that someone has to bring to your attention there are actually other possible outcomes to what you're doing. I know it can be difficult to comprehend this level of thinking." I jumped in quickly, "No no no no no no ... I know exactly what you're talking about. I experienced that once when I was in college."

It was my Junior year and I was running for SGA President. I had been Mr. Kentucky State University the year before and I was confident in the job I did and decided I could do even more if I was the actual student body President. So, I declared my candidacy, ran my campaign, and let the people know my aspirations and moved as if I was going to be President the following year. There were other people running but I LITERALLY did not even consider the thought of them winning because I KNEW the position was mine. The revelation of the level of thinking you're talking about came the night before the election. I was in my office writing down the initiatives I was planning to carry out the next year and one of my campaign volunteers came in and asked if I needed anything. I looked up and shook my head no. She said, "Ok." As she headed out, she stopped right before she crossed the threshold of the door and looked back and said, "Kobie, can I ask you something?" I put my pen down to give her my full attention and said, "Sure, shoot, go ahead." She said, "What are you going to do if you don't win?" I said, "Uh, I don't understand. What do you mean?" She said, "I mean if you lose the election?" I burst out laughing and said, "That's not going to happen!" There must have been a confidence and assurance in my tone that added a level of comfort that was absent before because she said, "Ok. I was a little worried." I replied, "Put your mind at ease and get ready to work this summer because we're going to have a lot to do to get ready for next year." She said, "Yes sir! Goodnight." And she walked out of the office. As I heard the door to the outside close behind her, I sat back in my chair and again burst out laughing. It hit me … that at NO POINT and I mean NONE AT ALL during the whole process from declaring to run, to putting together my team, to campaigning, to talking to students and asking them for their votes, including the debates and all the other stuff that goes along with running for an office, did I EVER and I mean EVER consider the fact of there being a possibility that I could lose. Not even in my private times by myself did the thought of losing EVER cross my mind. And at that moment, I was shocked, amazed, and almost in disbelief. I picked up the phone and called my girlfriend and said, "Babe, did you know there is a possibility I could lose?" She said, "Well, there are other people running but they don't stand a chance, and you really are the best person for the job." I said, "Awwww, thanks Babe. Yeah, that's what I was thinking, too!" She replied, "Boy, you are crazy. Get off my phone. Bye." And I hung up.

"YES!" he said excitedly. "That's it! Now you just have to live your WHOLE life that way. That confidence and that way of thinking should encompass your whole life. You shared with me you were trying to achieve this goal of making ten-fifteen thousand dollars a month. It's a good goal, but more than the money you have to think about what type of value you're going to offer." His cellphone rang and he looked down to read the number. He looked up at me and said, "Excuse me I have to take this. I'll be back shortly." He then stood up, and walked out of the room.

WIZISM

"You don't always get to choose the thoughts that come into your mind, but you do get to choose what stays."

WIZISM

"You need a picture of a process to help you maximize what you already have."

CHAPTER 2

Playing the Game to Win

---

*"There is no passion to be found in playing
small and settling for a life that is less than the
one you are capable of living."*
~Nelson Mandela

HE JUST DROPPED A BOMB THEN WALKED OUT of the
room. I'm kind of glad the phone call came when it did. I needed a
moment to try to process the totality of that statement. Live my
WHOLE life that way. How do I just live my WHOLE life that way?
Can you believe he just said live my WHOLE life that way? The

mindset and the way of being required to exist in that space seems way out of my reach and I don't even have a clue of what it would take to get there, and live there consistently day in and day out. Well, I guess that is not necessarily true. I'm thankful that I've at least experienced the level of thinking he's talking about if only for a brief moment in time. So, I guess it's not totally out of my reach. The capacity and ability I know reside within me and I have tangible proof. I'm at least hopeful the possibility of that reality may actually be within my reach.

As we live, I think we often tend to become comfortable in whatever space (mentally, physically, spiritually, economically or a combination of all) we are in, and often surround ourselves with people who are going to support and nurture that comfort, and are not going to push us too much to move out of those comfortable spaces. Most people don't intentionally put themselves in positions or situations they know are going to be uncomfortable and force growth. I had no idea this meeting was going to be one of those situations. This man just shook my whole world up and I don't think he was even trying to do it. He was just simply talking about his life and how he thinks and lives. He wasn't trying to impress me or puff himself up. He was just sharing his authentic life and trying to get me to understand his way of thinking and how it has caused him to arrive where he is currently. He was gracious enough to set aside two hours to talk to me and this was just the first thirty minutes. If this meeting ended right now, at this moment, I would have received a tremendous amount to chew on already. I had my note pad out and wrote down all the lessons and nuggets I felt were going to be valuable for later. I was excited to see what else I would be able to learn and glean from him as our conversation continued.

He walked back in the room and sat down and picked right up where he left off as if he'd never left at all. "Sorry about that. Thanks for understanding. So, you want to make more money and get to ten-fifteen thousand dollars a month? Right?" He looked at me and waited for a response. "Uh, yeah, right. Ten-fifteen thousand dollars a month," I replied nervously. I don't know if you have ever been in a room with someone and their very presence and energy made you feel small, but all of a sudden that's how I was feeling. Not because he said or did anything demeaning towards me, but it's as if when he left, he was a normal person like Clark Kent, and when he came back, he'd switched into his Superman outfit. Then entered the room with this aura of bigness that I couldn't physically see, but all of a sudden, I could feel it crowding me. I don't know if it was there the whole time and the last conversation just blew my mind so much that it caused me to interpret reality differently. All I know is now I'm questioning myself and I feel like I'm from Krypton, and I've been exposed to kryptonite and I'm feeling mighty weak. If I wasn't aware of his bigness before I feel it now at this moment and recognized it with the utmost clarity. I made sure I sat up straight, as I did not want to feel or look like I was physically shrinking as he spoke, "So how are you going to do that?" I looked at him and said, "Work harder!" That sounded like a good thing to say at the time. With me feeling like my superhero powers were fading, I for sure wasn't feeling really confident, so it definitely felt like the wrong answer. He looked at me as if trying to figure out something. He tilted his head slightly and said, "That's one way to go about it. But, specifically, what are you going to do? Don't feel like you have to answer the question right this moment, but know it is a question you are going to have to be able to answer in detail. We'll come back to it later and you're absolutely going to have to figure that out." I felt like I was in class and was asked for my homework that I knew I didn't do and was also about to be given a pop quiz on the same information. I was all types of nervous and anxious and didn't know why. He quickly shook his head as if he was answering something he asked himself and said, "Let's move on to something else that may actually help you answer that question when we come back to it. Let's talk about what makes you who you are, and what you believe."

"So, you want me to talk about who I am and what I believe?" I said quietly sounding really unsure of myself not really knowing what he was asking of me. "That's exactly what I want you to do!" He said with a smile on his face. "Uh, where do I start? Where do I start?" I looked up at the ceiling avoiding eye contact and stalling for time to try to come up with something profound to impress him. I got ready to open my mouth and before a word could come out he said, "I don't want you to tell me about your degrees or any titles you may have, I don't want to hear about what you do as a job or profession although we probably will eventually get around to why you do what you do. If you're married or have kids, I don't want to hear about those roles you operate in as a father or husband because those roles are not who you are. I'm talking about the concentrated, unadulterated, pure essence of you. If all that stuff was stripped away and you had no titles, if you didn't have a wife or kids (if you have them), and all the accolades and awards you have attained weren't there, who would you be?" He then smiled at me like we were playing chess and he had checkmate in two moves. He knows I can't stop it, and he's simply waiting for me to concede and lay down my king and say, "Good game." Then all of sudden, it's like my confidence was walking around the room blindly and found me and jumped back inside of me. Like someone came and removed the kryptonite out of the room and my powers were returning. I felt a rush of energy and sat up as if I heard my own personal theme music playing in the background and boldly said, "I am L. Kobie Wilkerson III, I am kind, loving, fun, honest, optimistic, hard-working, intelligent, patient, trustworthy, determined, faith-filled and resourceful!" He put both hands on his desk as if he was going to stand up and pushed himself back from his desk about 6 inches in his chair and clapped his hands twice and pointed at me and said energetically, "THAT'S IT! YOU GOT IT! You did it! Good job! I'm so excited for you. I know you're wondering what I am talking about. Well, first off, I saw you struggling and wrestling with what I was really asking of you, which is an appropriate posture to be in with that question. It is not an easy question to answer and most people give every answer but the correct one. It takes some honest introspection and familiarity with oneself to really get to the core of the character of a person.

See Kobie, success is fluid, and people have to define what it is and what it looks like for them personally. For some, they use money as a metric and others use awards or title attainment to measure their success. Some use accolades or social status to signify them making their mark. Disappointingly, the majority of those people, if you took whatever metric they used away from them, they'd feel like they were failures, or losers, or however they come to define the opposite of success is the box they'd put themselves in; and the fact of the matter is, it's simply not true. Often along the road or journey to success, people will trade or give small pieces of themselves away in exchange for the attainment of certain goals or achievements. A little compromise here, a bit of negotiation there, an ignoring of this, and looking of the other way with that, and then all of sudden they find themselves with all the stuff and prestige or fame or whatever metric they were using to chart and judge their success. They look around and don't even know who they are anymore, and they forget how they even got there. They begin to believe it's what they achieved that makes them who they are and fail to recognize or have forgotten it was the essence of who they were when they started their journey that allowed whatever metric they used for success to show up in the first place. It was them who made the difference, and somewhere along the road they began to feel like without the stuff they were nothing, and they failed to see the incredible value inside of them. This is why you hear the stories of famous people who seem to have it all committing suicide. Because in seeking to "gain it all," they lose sight of the thing most important to all of us, and that is knowing who you are and loving yourself. In order to love yourself, you have to first know yourself and have an honest open relationship with yourself. I mean the good and the parts about you that need work. You have to cultivate some beliefs that will carry you through the tough times that are destined to come if you are going to put forth an effort to live this life with some form of purpose and passion. Life is not supposed to be easy. If you want to play this game of life and win it, you have to understand the rules, and how to play the game and be clear about what it's going to take to come out on top. One of the utmost important things is recognizing who you are and what is in you! And NOBODY, and I mean NOBODY, can tell you that! Not your momma, or your grandma, or your spouse or your best friend, not your boss, or your kids, or your significant other, not your daddy or your siblings, or anyone! It's something you have to know and believe for yourself. Now don't get me wrong, people can see things in you and it's important to have people who can remind you of who you are, but if you don't first know it, and you don't first believe it, it doesn't matter how strong, loud, or passionate someone is about telling you about yourself. It just won't matter because you don't believe. See, what other people say and think about you means something, but what you think and say about yourself means EVERYTHING! That's why I got so excited when you told me who you were because I could tell when you said it you meant it and believed it. I was getting a little worried because I thought you were about to come to me with some crappy answer and I couldn't tell you what to say, and for the sake of time, I needed you to get there as quickly as possible. But I felt if I guided you a bit and got you in the neighborhood, you'd find the right house and come on in, and you did. Many people don't get to the correct answer really because of no fault of their own. Most people don't have conversations with others or themselves to force a magnified look inward. Also, lots of people don't have a good healthy relationship with themselves, and because of that, it's difficult to answer that specific question with any real sincerity or conviction. So, for you to process that question and get to the answer as soon as you did says a lot about you. It's exciting for me to meet other people who have a strong sense of who they are because then we can have a different conversation where we can talk on a level where ego doesn't exist, and we are not trying to one-up or outdo each other because of personal insecurities. In addition, I don't have to worry about there being blatant competition for attention in our conversation. People who know who they are don't have a problem celebrating others because they understand the light of life shining on other people doesn't diminish their chance to be in the light of life, or lessen their own internal light shining at all. The importance of knowing who you are is pertinent for personal and professional growth and the attainment of success. You don't just want to be successful. You want to be grounded and successful. The strong foundation for the manifestation of such success is knowledge and the understanding of self. But remember, the "knowing who you are" piece of the puzzle was only the first part of the question. The other part of the question was, "What do you believe?" His demeanor was very relaxed now, and I felt he was really about to share some extremely powerful stuff. I was feeling good too, like I got my mojo back. So, I knew the rest of our conversation was going to be exceptional, and on another level. I looked at him and said, "So let's dig deep into this belief thing. Give me what you got." He smiled and said, "I thought you were the one supposed to be answering the questions. I see what you're doing." And he pointed his finger at me and said, "Alright, I'll bite. Get your pen ready. I don't plan on repeating myself."

"We don't necessarily have time to dive into everything I'd like to cover regarding belief, but I'm going to give you the building blocks and I know you will be able to take it from there. Truthfully, I really want to hear from you, but we've now got a good foundation and I think you'll be able to openly receive the information I'm going to give you. More importantly, I believe you're in a position to apply it so you can continue your journey of forming a focused and winning mindset. On your pad there, take a blank sheet of paper and draw a line vertically to divide the paper in half, and then do the same thing horizontally so the paper will now be in four equal parts. At the top of each of those boxes, I want you to put one of these titles: faith, family, finances, and work. You got it?" I am writing as quickly as I possibly can. I hold up my notepad showing my four boxes and say, "Like this?" He shakes his head and replies, "Yes. Just like that. Now what you are going to do is in each of those boxes you are going to put what you believe about each of those things. Be thoughtful and honest as you compose each list because if you aren't then you only hurt yourself in the process. You have to tell the truth to yourself about yourself. If you want the mindset this is part of the process." I begin writing my list in my first box faith. He interrupts me. "What are you doing?" I look up at him and say, "I'm composing my list." He chuckles a little and shakes his head. "Kobie we don't have the time for you to do that now. You're going to have to do this tough work on your time so it can be thoughtful and not rushed. Right now, I am giving you the instructions so you will know what to do once you get home. I need you to make sure you do the work and you do this part of the exercise first." I look at him and point at him with my pen in hand and say, "Got it." He continued on. "Now take the paper from the bottom and fold it upwards to fold it in half. At the top (which is the bottom of the backside of the paper) you're going to write, "I Believe I am…" and then on this side you are going to write the things you believe about yourself currently. You're going to put all the positive things you believe about yourself on the top half of the sheet and then flip it over and on the bottom half, you're going to put those not so favorable things you believe about yourself. On the inside of the paper, you have what you believe about faith, family, finances, and work, but all of those beliefs at some level are traced back to what you believe about yourself. See, people think to change themselves they have to create new habits and behaviors, so their actions are different, and yeah that's an important piece of it. But the actions come from somewhere. The roots that give life to the actions are your beliefs. Why you do what you do is all because you ultimately believe something. I really would like to go deeper but we don't have time. Just make sure you follow directions and do it in the order I told you. Complete the faith, family, finances, and work part first, and then fold it up and do the part about you; the good beliefs and the beliefs that need a little work and attention. The short of it is people want to take shortcuts to a long process and you can do that, but understand the outcome won't be the same. I need you to be aware that most people don't really know what they believe deeply and that's why it's so difficult and such a laborious chore for them to change and master life. And my friend, you are most people. And the bigger issue is most people don't think they are most people, and that is why the change in their life doesn't show up because they feel like they don't have to do the work necessary to become more. They run from it instead of towards it. It's in facing the things you want to run from and understanding why you're running from it that you become better. If you feel a little offended it's a natural response to truth. Feel it and embrace it. We don't get to be better until we are honest with ourselves and our natural response is to defend or justify. Remember that when you are in church or in conversations with other people and they say something that causes the feeling of offense to rise up in you. Take a moment and ask yourself, is there any truth in it, and deal with that. In the end, I promise it makes you better. But anyway, if you felt a little offended or not, the important thing is you make sure when you get home you do this work. Got it?" I looked at him and replied strongly, "Got it!" He stood up and said, "I'm going to go grab a water. I'll bring you one too." And he walked out of his office.

WIZISM

"Do not take a short cut to a long process and expect your intended outcome!"

WIZISM

"To do something you have never done before, you are going to have to do some things you have never done before!"

CHAPTER 3

Figuring It Out: Solving Problems

*"When facing a problem and trying to figure
it out the only way to find out is to get into
action and find out." ~L. Kobie Da Wiz
(Wizism)*

AS HE LEFT THE ROOM, I BEGAN TO WRITE on my notepad
some intuitive take-aways I was getting from the conversation we just
had:

Life itself is a series of challenges and problems you are meant
to face and overcome. The challenges and problems that come

to you are meant to make you, not break you. They are designed to make you better and give you lessons to learn so you can live powerfully in your present and craft the future you desire. Often, you get overwhelmed because when you choose to ignore one problem or challenge you can fail to realize not addressing it doesn't make it go away. In fact, it only exacerbates your life. So why do you ignore or not face what's presented to and for you? You don't face it because of fear of failing, lack of confidence, laziness, not wanting to do the work, seeking to avoid conflict, and a host of other reasons. Whatever the reasons are you must get beyond them and turn and begin to run towards what you've been running from.

I'm trying to process all the powerful information he just gave me. I'm glad he's taking these small breaks because I need them to get my head together. I'm getting some amazing stuff from what he is saying, and I think I'm getting even more from what he's not saying. This is important when in conversations with people. You have to recognize and be present in the conversation being had in front of you, but you also have to be aware of the things that are being transferred and communicated but aren't really being said. I call it the background conversation. It's important and not to be overlooked. It's closely tied to a saying you may have heard that states, "What's understood doesn't need to be spoken." He is speaking some STUFF! But, it's also in what he is not saying that I'm gleaning from too. I'm going to need to take a two-day personal retreat just to get my mind around all of this information. I've only been here an hour and it feels like I've been here all day. Not in a bad way, or this dragging on kind-of-way, but in I've gotten so much out of it in such a short time it feels like time has slowed down and I've been here longer than I have. Honestly, I feel a bit mentally exhausted trying to process it all. I think I'm going to need a nap after this. Listening and thinking is hard work and takes a lot of energy. I hear him coming back down the hall. If this dude comes back in here with even more of an aura than he did last time I don't know if I'll be able to take it.

He walks back in and hands me a bottle of water. I say, "Thanks, I appreciate it." We open our bottles at the same time and take a drink almost in sync. I'm waiting to see if I feel any energy fluctuations, but it seems as if everything is the same. "Whew!" I sighed out loud. He said, "What is it?" I put the cap on my water bottle and said, "Oh it's nothing. Just processing everything." I didn't want to say I am glad you didn't come back in here glowing like a Super Saiyan. He takes his bottle of water and drinks the whole thing, places the top back on and crushes it between his hands. "Now, where were we?" And he looks at me and rubs his hands together like Mr. Miyagi in Karate Kid and goes, "Ah yes, and now back to our regularly scheduled program. I didn't forget. Ten-fifteen thousand dollars a month." Ah man, I'm thinking to myself. Here is the pop quiz I was dreading. But now after the previous conversations, I felt a bit better prepared to answer it than I did before. He looks at me and slightly smirks and says, "Are you ready to tell me how you are going to get to the goal you set of ten-fifteen thousand dollars a month?" I look back at him and confidently say, "Well ready or not here I come."

I took a deep breath wanting to be sure to pick my words carefully. I began slowly, "Well, before we had the previous conversations, I simply said work harder. I now know you wanted a much deeper answer. I am going to say before I figure out how I'm going to get to the mark of ten-fifteen thousand dollars a month I probably want to be clear on my beliefs about finances/money and my beliefs about work. I clearly haven't sat down and done all of that work yet. But, I know for sure a few of my beliefs concerning them. I believe money is a tool used to build things, so the question is what is the ten-fifteen thousand dollars going to be used to create. I also believe money is abundant and I should shift my focus to being open to receiving more money as opposed to focusing on my lack of it. In regard to work, I believe my focus should be working to learn more than about earning money. I also believe in working I should be intentional about adding value to the spaces and places I occupy. I also believe when it comes to work I should put myself in positions where I can share my gifts and talents and look to enhance them whenever possible. "Very good." He said. "Now keep going and put those pieces together and tell me what you're able to come up with." I sat there looking down for about 45 seconds, which felt like forever and said nothing. I heard the creaking in his chair. He is twisting slowly side to side waiting patiently for me to speak. I slowly raise my head and say, "I think what I am supposed to be coming up with is my ability to increase my income is going to be directly connected to what I believe about money, work, and myself. Whether I realize it or not, what I believe comes to manifest in my life; and if what I desire is not showing up then I need to take a look at my beliefs and consider changing those so my actions and behaviors will all be in line. Doing that will allow me to live a truer and more authentic life. In addition, my understanding and application of this puts me in a position of power to really take control of my life. It helps me to be the solution to issues and not look to blame others for problems or situations that ultimately may be within my realm of control." He looked at me and said, "Very good grasshopper." We both chuckled. He folded his arms on his desk and leaned forward and said, "Now I can tell you what I wanted to tell you when you first asked me that question, but you weren't ready to receive the answer which was this. You're not going to be able to make ten-fifteen thousand dollars a month until you believe that you can. And the moment you believe you can, you'll start to pull it towards you in your thoughts and your actions will fall in line. I want you to remember this as well: To do something you've never done before, you're going to have to do some things you've never done before. You don't get to the place of more or better by doing the same! Do you know why I make the money I make? Because I believe I can, and I have put myself in a position to do so with my thoughts, beliefs, actions, and behaviors. I have also committed to doing my part of the work necessary to complete the equation. I expect the money to show up because I have done the things that I know I must do, and then I give the universe multiple ways to get the money to me. You have to be intentional about things you do and how you choose to spend your time because you only have so much time, and contrary to the statement "time is money," time is more important than money because you can find additional ways to get more money, but the time you have is finite. You're trying to get to the level of ten-fifteen thousand dollars a month. You're aware from our mastermind group we have people at all different levels of income. If I only made ten-fifteen thousand dollars a month I'd be in a world of hurt. Ten-fifteen thousand dollars a month is what I pay for feed for my horses. That doesn't include boarding them and the other expenses that arise just for them. I have living expenses and a payroll that tops out at about 140K/month. What you have to deal with is different than what I have to deal with, but we both have stuff we have to deal with. You have problems and situations you have to address, and so do I, and everyone else does as well. For me, it's about keeping my purpose, passion, perspective, and priorities all in check. I look at it as the places I've intentionally aspired to and every level I graduate to allows me to increase my impact and expand my purpose. As I add value to the planet, I exchange the value I provide for the money. We are all playing the same game, but the levels at which we are playing are just not the same. Doesn't mean you can't aspire and figure out how to get to my level, and it doesn't mean I won't ever find myself back at your level. This is what I love about the diversity of our mastermind group. No matter what level you're on you can always learn something from someone else. The moment you get too big for your britches and you feel like you know it all is the moment to prepare yourself for the fall that's coming. Gratefulness and thankfulness are how one should choose to live their life. Because once you realize all the stuff can go quicker than it came, you reach a plane of understanding where you realize what is in you is what is most important, and that is what you have to protect at all cost.

So, knowing who you are and what you believe is important as you climb the mountain of life and chart your path to the top; but it is even more important should you fall off that mountain and have to climb back up it again. Do you understand what I'm saying?" I looked at him with a firm determined look and said, "I believe I understand exactly what you are saying." He clasped his hands together and looked at his watch and said, "Good then. I don't think I need to say any more about that."

WIZISM

"What other people say and think about you means something, but what you think and say about yourself means EVERYTHING!"

WIZISM

"It's in facing the things you want to run from and understanding why you're running from it that you become better."

CHAPTER 4

Going for More: Building Your Bridges

"When you know better you have an OPPORTUNITY to do better! Knowing alone doesn't guarantee you will get into action and exercise what you know. It's in the doing you get your power." ~L. Kobie Da Wiz (Wizism)

I SAT BACK IN MY CHAIR AND ASKED him a question: "How long do you think you've had the mindset that has allowed you to operate at this level?" "Wow, Kobie that's a good question. If I'd had to guess I'd say I think I've always felt I had the capacity for it since probably my junior year in college. I had glimpses and flashes of it as you did, but I don't think the level of operation we're discussing showed up and became somewhat of a permanent piece of my being until the end of my surgery residency. I can't narrow it down exactly, but sometime between the ages of 33-35. About 20 years I've been blessed to carry this mindset and operate in it now without hesitation. I've been doing it so long I almost don't remember how to think any other way. I remember how I operated before I started to fully embrace this mindset and I can definitely tell you I like this way a lot better. The benefits of this mindset include an elevated level of confidence and assurance that you already know can't fully be explained. As well as the ability to look at problems and solve them quicker and at a much higher level. And because of those things your faith increases so you don't hesitate, and you move more decisively. The benefits far outweigh the work it takes to develop this mindset. But let me be transparent in stating that it requires a lot more maintenance, and a level of effort than most people are willing to put forth. In order to keep this mindset in operation you have to fight against a great deal of negativity and doubt that comes at you on a regular basis. But, over time it becomes habitual; how you fend off certain thoughts and feelings that come to try to steal your power. You could definitely say it feels a bit like being a super-hero."

His office phone rang, and he picked up fairly quickly. "Hello." He twisted side to side in his chair in a way where you could tell he did it quite often. He listened intently and then said, "Really, funny you say that. I actually have the exact person you need to speak to right here in my office. Your timing is perfect. Hold on for one second." He put the phone on hold and then looked at me and said, "I need you to do me a favor." I looked at him with a slight look of bewilderment and said, "Sure how can I help." He leaned over his desk, "This is my nephew John on the phone and he's calling me because he said he feels stuck. He's in college and often needs some direction. You know how that is. He checks in with me from time to time seeking advice and a positive push, or a pat on the back, but I think he'll receive it better if it comes from you. He just needs a little bit of encouragement and I think you have something he needs." Man, how could I say no to that? "Well, put him on, and let's see what the Universe has for him." He took the call off hold and put him on speaker. "Hey, John are you there?" "Yeah, I'm here." Smiling at me and gave me two thumbs up. "I have a friend of mine here and we've been having some conversations about growth and being better. Our conversations are a bit deeper than the ones you and I normally have as uncle and nephew, but you're growing to a place where you'll be able to swim in these deep waters with us soon. We still have a bit more time left in our meeting, but I wanted to take a few minutes to try to get you in a better place. You know what I believe about family right?" He looked at me and winked, "Yes, Sir. You believe family is most important and if we can't make time for family then we only hurt ourselves. You believe in helping family out but not living our lives for us. You believe people have to be free to make their own choices." He's smiling ear to ear and you can tell he has drilled that into his nephew. "You're exactly right, and that's why I do my best to always make time for you. So, my friend Kobie is going to give you some words of encouragement, and then we're going to get back to our meeting. I want you to just listen to what he has to say. I know it's going to be exactly what you need."

"Hey, John, I'm L. Kobie Da Wiz and your uncle told me you were feeling a little stuck. Is that right?" "Yeah, that's it. I'm feeling like I just don't know where I want to be." I scoot up to the edge of my seat and say, "Well, the only thing separating you from where you are, and where you want to be is simply something you don't know. You have the knowledge to figure this out. Knowledge is the bridge to your destiny, and you have to cross it if you want to get there. Credit is given to Dr. Maya Angelo for the quote, "Do the best you can until you know better. Then when you know better, you do better." But in practice, the reality of that quote is not necessarily true. The L. Kobie Da Wiz Wizism is, "When you know better you have an OPPORTUNITY to do better!" Knowledge provides the opportunity. Whether you take advantage of the opportunity is going to be up to you. And from just having this brief meeting with your uncle, I know you know some stuff. When I was growing up, I loved watching the cartoon "G.I. Joe: The Great American Hero." The cartoon was known for the famous saying, "Knowing is half the battle! YO JOE!" What they didn't tell you and what was insinuated was that you knew what the other half of the battle was. The other half of the battle where the war is won is in DOING what you know to do! That's where the power to shift and turn your life around happens. It's in doing something you already know. So, John, I want you to take a bit of an inventory and think about what you know, and how you can move from this place of uncertainty. I bet if you took a few minutes and thought about what you really want to do, then make a decision and move, you'll find yourself feeling better in no time." There was a pause and silence on the phone. I said, "You there, John?" Then we heard a voice on the other end. "That was very helpful." His uncle jumped in. "Alright nephew, put those words into practice and get to doing." He winked at me. "Ok, Unc. I'll talk to you later. Thanks, Mr. Da Wiz. I appreciate the encouragement." I jumped in smiling. "It was my pleasure." He hung up the phone and said, "Thank you for that. That was amazing. I guess you've given a speech or two in your lifetime huh?" I looked at him and sat back, "Maybe one or two." He then continued, "But seriously, I knew you'd knock it out the park. But I didn't think he was going to get all of that. You really gave him some real-life advice to keep him going for a good while. I got something out of that too. YO JOE!" He said emphatically as he started laughing. "You're a really good speaker. I feel honored to have been able to see you in action. You're not going to send me an invoice after this are you? I mean if you do, I guess I'd be obligated to pay it. That was some real Les Brown type of speaking." I jumped in chuckling. "Naw, I'm not going to charge you this time. I'm honored that you trusted me with your family. I heard how much family means to you and I see you have shared your beliefs with him to the point where he knows what you believe by heart. I'm going to give you that one on the house. I'm thankful you recognized and believed in my talent and skills enough to put me on the spot and believe I'd deliver. Funny you mention Les Brown. Believe it or not I actually went through his speaker training program, so that's a real compliment. I guess some of it actually rubbed off on me." He looked a bit astonished, "Are you serious?" "As a heart attack," I said. "I was already impressed by you, but that gives me even more reason to feel as though I'm in the company of a really special person. Well, let's continue on and get you the last pieces of this puzzle."

"Well now you have the tools to get your beliefs in order. Let's talk about putting this knowledge into practice and as you told my nephew, doing what you know to do. I'm going to give you a few words and if you can find it in yourself to do what is necessary to embody these words, I promise there will be nothing you won't be able to accomplish or attain. Words have power! The words you allow to live in you and through you will make the difference in your life, and in the lives of others. The words I want you to hold onto and really work to embody are, discipline, consistency, and follow-through. These are the three things you have to master if you want to hold on to the mindset we've been talking about. What did you tell my nephew? Knowing gives you the opportunity to do better. Most people know these words and most people partly embody them. They may be good at disciplining themselves when it comes to eating right or exercising and that's good. But how good are they at disciplining their thoughts? That's what I'm talking about. When I speak of discipline, consistency, and follow-through, I'm talking about taking control of what you think and speak first, and then what you do. Most people start with the actions and you know from our conversations today that's only the fruit of the tree. The most important part of the tree you can't even see. That's the part I want you to spend the majority of your energy tending to and taking care of. Whatever you have to do to protect your mind, take those steps and don't apologize to anyone for it. If you don't take the time to do what you need to do for you, then don't be disappointed when others don't either. You have to walk the tightrope of selfishness and selflessness and learn to read situations to know which of the two is required. You definitely have to help yourself so you can have the capacity to help others. You have to be what you're trying to be before you actually become it. Let me give you an example. People fall in love and have the desire to get married. The man asks the woman to be his wife and they become engaged. If either of them waits until the day of the wedding to start being the husband or the wife, the marriage is going to fail. You don't want to wait to start operating as a husband or wife the day you get married. You actually have to become that before you get married. People don't often realize the actual achievement of a thing happens before the achievement is acknowledged. The work put in to earning the distinction gets you the win before it actually shows up. Do you want to be the best at something? Then start being the best now and doing what you think the best would do. The mental fortitude it takes to be something before everybody else sees it, takes a belief and a strength very few people are capable of holding onto and carrying out. Do you know what it takes for that to happen? Discipline, consistency, and follow-through! The story of Noah building a boat on dry land for an event that NEVER happened before is an example of what I am talking about. It NEVER rained! The dew came up from the ground to water the plants because what's the most important part of the plant? Uh huh! Yep! The roots, baby! But every day for YEARS he built and he built and the people talked about him. Every single day he still built and worked on his vision because he believed in it. Do you know what that takes? YEP! Discipline, consistency, and follow-through. To some people those are just words. For you to have this mindset it has to become the essence of who you are. Not just because you say it, but because you live it and it shows up in everything you do. Once you get familiar with your beliefs to the point where, just like my nephew, you can recite them by heart, then you can go for more. And you know how you go for more? It's going to take discipline, consistency, and follow-through. Now once you have those down, you have to add optimism and resilience and then you'll be unstoppable. The optimism and resilience won't serve you if you don't have the discipline, consistency and follow-through. Without those things, your optimism becomes false hope, and your resilience morphs into frustration. And let me tell you this, my friend, there is almost nothing worse than those two things for one's mindset. Nothing works against you more than frustration and false hope, which is why you must be vigilant in your discipline, unrelenting in your consistency, and persistent in your follow-through when it comes to your thinking and operating in your beliefs. These, my friend, are the essential keys to your success. Now I have one last piece to the puzzle I want to give you. With this piece, you'll be well equipped with enough of the tools to move you on to creating and cultivating this mindset for yourself."

WIZISM

"Time is more important
than money because you
can find additional ways to
get more money, but the
time you have is finite."

WIZISM

"Don't focus so much on success and failure; those are judgments upon which we often attach too much meaning. Focus on the process; that's where we get our power."

CHAPTER 5

Living Vs Staying Alive

"You are the main character in the story of your life. You don't have control of all the climaxes and falls of the story. But, as much as you can, make sure you are the one who is holding the pen and that you're writing a story you will be proud of!"
~L. Kobie Da Wiz (Wizism)

"SO KOBIE, IF YOU COULD GIVE ME ONE NUGGET that is a takeaway but something that I didn't say, but you know it's definitely part of this conversation, what would that be?" Without hesitation and as if I already had it written down in anticipation I said, "Don't focus so much on success and failure; those are judgments upon which we often attach too much meaning. Focus on the process; that's where we get our power." He looked at me with his eyes wide open and said, "Man that is beyond excellent! My friend, that is an astounding intuitive nugget and a great observation. I hope you have enjoyed this time with me as much as I have with you. I can honestly say you have made my day. I am so glad I took this meeting. Honestly, I almost didn't. Not because I was trying to avoid you or anything like that, but because I had a meeting with a rep from a surgical company that is seriously considering helping me to patent a tool and process I've created for wrist replacement. They ended up canceling and now I firmly believe this time was meant for you. No, let me correct that. It was meant for us. So, I went from having no time to meet to an open solid 2-hour block of time that was destined for us. I want to thank you for your persistence in making this meeting happen because these two hours have not only shown me how amazing you are, but they also unlocked some things in me. As I was guiding you to a place of self-reflection, I was forced to think about the best way to help you see what you needed to see. In helping you become better, I also became better in the process. I got just as much out of this as you did. Maybe even more. I know for a fact you have shifted to another level. The speed at which you snapped off the intuitive nugget let me know your radar and awareness is not at the same place it was when you first came into this office. We have taken a journey over these last two hours and I want you to leave with this last and very important lesson.

I want to have a conversation about living vs staying alive. Or we can say living vs existing. But I prefer staying alive for this reason. Staying alive represents just surviving and that's the enemy I want to face and make sure you do everything you can to avoid. Staying alive is a space of low energy and despair. It's a space that is uninspiring and drains you of faith, hope, and light. It kills creativity and lacks purpose and passion. This is not the space you want to wake up and find yourself in day after day. Staying alive and the mindset that goes along with it places you in a hole where the level of difficulty to escape on a scale of 1-10 approaches 10. Beware of people who are just staying alive because they will pull you into the black hole of despair and the attitude of self-deprivation will possess you and you won't even know it. Saying all that, I will say as long as you are alive, you have a chance to really LIVE, and if you have to reside there until someone can come to save you, or until you can muster enough power and energy to save yourself, then do that. Now, let's talk about really living.

If you don't take anything else from this conversation that we've had, I want you to remember this main thing: You have the power to create the life you want regardless of where you have come from and regardless of your current situation. Your demographics don't determine your destiny and your present situation is not your forever outcome. Your situation can change as soon as your mindset does. Make every effort to give yourself the mental space to allow yourself to be successful. It is the greatest gift you can give to yourself. I want to talk about a strategy you can use to give yourself the mental space to be great. Remember earlier when I made the statement time is finite?" I looked at him and said, "I absolutely do remember when you said that." "Well let me tell you how you can actually buy yourself some time. I call it living in my future. What I do is take account of my monthly expenses and try as best I can to have them paid 6 months in advance, and then try to save 6 months. That's part of the game I play. Let me share the benefit of this when we are talking about having this mindset we've been discussing. When you do that, you basically give yourself the space to fail without serious consequence. When you know your major bills are all paid up 6 months in advance, you have the mental space and the financial space to take risks and fail. And, you know your place of residence and your other bills are going to be covered for 180 days. That is a tremendous gift to give yourself and your family. You sleep differently when your bills are paid up 6 months in advance. You operate in a different space attitude-wise when your bills are paid up 6 months in advance. Your confidence level goes up and you need your confidence at a high level if you are going to manifest this mindset in a real way. And just like we discussed earlier, the levels at which we live this life vary. So, for my businesses, I need about 1.2 -1.5 million to have my 6 months paid up, and the same for 6 months of reserve. Right now, I have my 6 months in advance set aside and am working on my 6 months of reserve. This is part of what living looks like. I believe money is a tool to build security for me and the ones I love, and that's how I use it. Do you see how my beliefs dictate my actions and my behaviors to create the life I want? Living is about deciding what you want, why you want it, and then going after it with a tenacity that is frightening. Living is determining your path to happiness and then aggressively pursuing it because it's what you want.

There is something I briefly touched on earlier in our conversations but wanted to make sure you didn't miss it, and that is talking to yourself. This is part of Living vs Staying Alive. Talking through things with yourself at least gives you a chance to hear what is going on. Learning happens through conversations, and sometimes that conversation needs to be between you and yourself. Don't feel bad about it or think you are crazy. Sometimes you need to get another person's opinion and that is helpful. But, a lot of times, your opinion is the only opinion you need. Trust yourself enough to be wise enough to give yourself objective advice and not just the advice you want to hear. This is necessary for living a successful life! It's not so much the ability to have the conversation, but the courage to trust yourself to make decisions that are going to be in your best interest." Is this making sense for you?" I looked at him and said, "It definitely makes sense. I'm listening and taking it all in." He continued on, "I feel a little bit like I'm rambling. I just want to make sure I don't forget anything. I know we can simply have other meetings, but I know how my schedule is. I can literally count on my 2 hands the last time in three years I had 2 hours free in the middle of the week. So, I'm not saying this won't happen again, but I'm saying it's going to require work to make it happen again like this. This was definitely a divine appointment for both of us. Is there anything you want to share with me before we depart from each other?" I pulled out my phone, "Actually there is.

I've been processing these last two hours and know that when I leave here the universe is going to test me to see how bad I really want this. I'm nervous, anxious and excited because I know from these last two hours I am a different person. As I go over my notes when I leave here and over the next few days, I know I'm going to be moved closer to the space of how you said earlier of living my WHOLE life this way. That excites me, but I know it's not going to come easy, and so before I leave I want to share this poem I wrote a little while ago that is definitely applicable to what I am getting ready to encounter:

"A Little Bit at a Time"

A Little Bit at a Time

A little bit at a time is how change and transformation come. I need to do one hundred things, but I must start with one.

A little bit at a time is what I tell myself, I must be the loudest voice in my life regardless of everybody else.

A little bit at a time creates the possibility of success, I can focus on doing better and relieve some of my stress.

A little bit at a time is the mantra I speak, when things get bad or life is seeming a little bleak.

A little bit at a time is the best way I know, to walk my talk, and let my actions show.

A little bit at a time is how to make it through the pain, it's how I smile in the trouble and appreciate the rain.

So, when life gets hard and I really want to quit, I dig down deep and say, "Just give a little bit!"

When I'm in a storm and don't know what to do, when giving up seems easy and I don't want to see it through; When my head is down and it seems too heavy to lift, I whisper to myself "Just give a little bit!"

A little bit, a little bit, is all I need to start. It doesn't stop there but it gets me out the dark.

A little bit, a little bit keeps me in the game. It won't fix everything, but it is what begins the change.

Keep the faith, see it through, and refuse to give up is what I must do.

I'll speak it in my heart and speak it in my mind and say out-loud to myself "A little bit at a time!"

A little bit at a time, a little bit at a time, all I have to do is a little bit at a time.

-L. Kobie Da Wiz

"So, I thank you for your time and as I get ready to go out here and chase this mindset, I'm going to do it a little bit at a time." "Wow, Kobie, you continue to impress me. Just when I think you've shown me your hand you pull something else out of the bag. That poem is incredible. Please make sure you email me a copy so I can have it framed and put it on the wall here in my office and at home. That poem will definitely help me and others to get on the other side of whatever we are going through." We both stood up and he walked me to the door. "Kobie it has been an absolute pleasure!" I reached out my hand to shake his hand, "No sir, the pleasure has been all mine. And I mean that!" I walked down the hall to the elevator and pushed the down button. I looked back and he was still standing in the hall. The elevator doors opened. I stepped in and waved as the doors closed. He yelled, "Do that work!" What a day I thought to myself. I can definitely say I didn't know what this day was going to hold. But man, I'm super glad it went the way it did. Man, oh man, did I get some lessons to help me master this game of life.

WIZISM

"What you and a lot of other people don't REALLY know is your secret sauce and magical ingredient in putting together your potion of success is YOU and your strong belief in your skills and abilities."

DAY 8 NOTES (8/29/20)

I got a full night's sleep and as I get ready to look over the book for final revisions, I was told I could only add to the introduction and here. The book is not to be changed (allowing only for light revisions of grammar and spelling). I've been thinking about doing a side-note piece to add some further insight to the why behind some of my decisions, but seeing I have to have the book uploaded fairly quickly, I doubt that is going to manifest right this moment. But, be on the lookout for some resources to help you take a deeper dive into the information. Oh, and the audio book will be released too. I'm also planning to put some journal entries and other behind the scenes stuff in that, so make sure you grab it. I just opened up my Facebook page and got a memory, ya'll I can't make this up ...

Facebook post 8/29/13

> "What a difference a day makes! Won't go into all of it, but I will say this...Trust in what's in you! The time and energy you've taken to grow your skills, gifts & talents isn't in vain. MORE than what you're waiting for will show up! You're the answer to somebody's prayer, and vice versa! #keepthefaith #dontquit #presson"

Y'all that was 7 years ago. Coincidence? I think not. I wrote that post 7 years ago to the day. And it's not by chance that it speaks to me to confirm a miracle process that took me 7 days. I don't know what you take from it, but I take from it the timelessness of Spirit and that there is power and blessings in obedience.

I'm so thankful to have been able to be used. I did not read the whole book until this morning. I finished chapter 5 last night (at 11:56pm) and just closed my computer. I didn't even read it. I was mentally and spiritually exhausted.

I think it's important you all know this book came from scratch. I had ideas only, but NOTHING was written until 8/22/20. I didn't have the direction of the book until day three (late Monday night). I didn't finish chapter one until four days in (late Tuesday night). I was worried and didn't think I was going to be able to accomplish this miracle. But if something is brought to you, then it's for you. So, I had to have a conversation with myself and reminded myself if GOD trusted me to assign it to me, and gave me the vision, He would provide the provision to see it to its completion. Some of you just finished reading this and feel like you have some big things you are trying to achieve and accomplish, and you are feeling like it's not going to happen. KEEP GOING! The ONLY way to a thing is to go THROUGH some things! Trust in your skills, and abilities, and believe in you and what you're doing until ALL doubt disappears. DO it for the people it's going to benefit and remove the ego of self and the sense of accomplishment from the equation. It's not about you. Approach it from that perspective and you'll witness an ease that will appear as you continue through your process.

Thank you for purchasing this book. If it empowered, motivated, or helped you out at all, think of some people you know who need the messages and the energy of these words and send them a copy of this book. I was only a vessel for what showed up on these pages. I DARE NOT take credit for writing this book. I wrote this book, but believe me when I tell you I DID NOT WRITE this book (those who get it, get it!). Open yourself up and put yourself in a space to be used by the Universe. It is in us all and runs through us all. Live your life on purpose with passion and intention so you may die empty is my eternal prayer for you.

#Learninghappensthroughconversations is the hashtag I want you to use to share out your insights and take-aways with your friends and the world. Help me expand these important conversations we need to have so we can all be the best versions of ourselves. I'll be looking for your input. Thanks for sharing.

...

Stay connected to us through the Learning Happens Through Conversations website at:

www.LearningHappensThroughConversations.com

WIZISM

"Your belief in you has to be unshakeable to the point where it may almost be perceived as arrogance."

WIZISM

"A faith that can be seen and touched really isn't faith at all; and a faith that hasn't been tested is a faith that can't be trusted!"

ABOUT THE AUTHOR

L. Kobie Wilkerson a.k.a L. Kobie Da Wiz is an award-winning author, poet, speaker, presenter, storyteller, edutainer, master teacher, and powerful transformer of schools and organizations. He ingeniously converts resistance to change into receptiveness for growth. He is a leading authority on helping schools and organizations cultivate relationships that support a healthy culture and climate. Kobie works with schools and organizations where it is his goal to see them systematically operate at their best, so they can effectively impact those they serve.

Passionate about continuous growth, he decided to pursue education to shape and mold the values of children by inspiring them to love knowledge and to be lifelong learners. Mr. Wilkerson has a B.A. in Education and a B.S. in Sociology from Kentucky State University. He obtained his Masters in Education Administration from Kansas State University. Kobie was also selected as a South Carolina Educational Policy Fellow, a program of the Institute for Educational Leadership out of Washington, D.C. Kobie is a graduate of the Les Brown speaker training institute, and has also completed the ACT Life Leadership Coaching program. In addition, he is also a certified John Maxwell Coach and Trainer.

Paperback and eBooks available on Amazon.com

For hardback copies, please visit www.lkobiedawiz.com